Figgis Surname

Ireland: 1600s to 1900s

From Ireland Church Records of Baptism, Marriage and Death

Comprised of Roman Catholic and Church of Ireland Records

From Counties Carlow, Cork, Kerry and Dublin City

Compiled by **Donovan Hurst**

March 12, 2012

Dedication

This work is dedicated to all of those that came before us and shaped our lives to make us the people that we are today.

Table of Contents

Introduction

This is a compilation of individuals who have the surname of Figgis that lived in the country of Ireland from the 1600s to the 1900s. I have placed each entry into one of four categories: Families, Individual Births/Baptisms, Individual Burials, and Individual Marriages. If a marriage entry primarily concerns an Individual Figgis who is female, then I have placed that entry under the category of Individual Marriages. If a marriage entry primarily concerns an Individual Figgis who is male, then I have placed that entry under the category of Families. Images of many of these listings are available at http://churchrecords.irishgenealogy.ie/churchrecords/.

To help guide the reader of this work, the format of this book is as follows:

- Main Family Entry (Husband and Wife) (Father and Mother)

  o Child of Main Family Entry, including Spouse(s) when available

    ▪ Grandchild of Main Family Entry, including Spouse(s) when available

      • Great-Grandchild of Main Family Entry, including Spouse(s) when available

(**Bolded Text**) following any entry includes any additional information such as Residence(s), Occupation(s), Signature(s), etc. when available.

Hurst

Some of the fonts used in this work symbolizes Celtic writing. The traditional letters, numbers, and punctuation marks and their Celtic counterparts are as follows:

Traditional Letters (Uppercase & Lowercase)

A a B b C c D d E f G g H h I i J j K k L l M m N n O o P p Q q R r S s T t U u V v W w X x Y y Z z

Celtic Letters (Uppercase & Lowercase)

A a B b C c D ð E e F ƒ G g H h I í J j K k L l M m

N n O o P p Q q R r S s T t U u V v W w X x Y y Z z

Traditional Numbers

1 2 3 4 5 6 7 8 9 10

Celtic Numbers

1 2 3 4 5 6 7 8 9 10

Traditional Punctuation

. , : ' " & - ( )

Celtic Punctuation

. , : ' " & - ( )

Parish Churches

Dublin (Church of Ireland)

Clontarf Parish, Harold's Cross Parish, Leeson Park Parish, Rathmines Parish, St. Catherine Parish, St. Mary Parish, St. Nicholas Without Parish, and St. Peter Parish.

Dublin (Roman Catholic or RC)

Rathmines Parish, St. Catherine Parish, and St. Mary, Pro Cathedral Parish.

ℱamilies

- Charles Figgis & Augusta Figgis

  - Ellen Augusta Figgis – b. 3 Apr 1897, bapt. 30 May 1897 (Baptism, **Leeson Park Parish**)

Charles Figgis (father):

   Residence - 70A Upper Leeson Street - May 30, 1897

   Occupation - Tea Merchant - May 30, 1897

- George Alexander Figgis & Harriet Unknown

Signature:

  - William Henry Rothschild Figgis – b. 27 Jun 1868, bapt. 8 Jan 1869 (Baptism, **Rathmines Parish**)

  - Marion Keene Figgis & Robert Johnston – 3 Nov 1900 (Marriage, **Clontarf Parish**)

Signatures:

Marion Keene Figgis (daughter):

Residence - Glenbrook Howth Road, Clontarf - November 3, 1900

Robert Johnston, son of Robert Johnston (son-in-law):

Residence - Alexandra's House Ball's Bridge, Dublin - November 3, 1900

Occupation - Bank of Ireland - November 3, 1900

Robert Johnston (father):

Occupation - Barrister at Law

George Alexander Figgis (father):

Occupation - Bank of Ireland

Wedding Witnesses:

J. Johnston, John Connell, George A. Figgis, and George H. Marsh

Signatures:

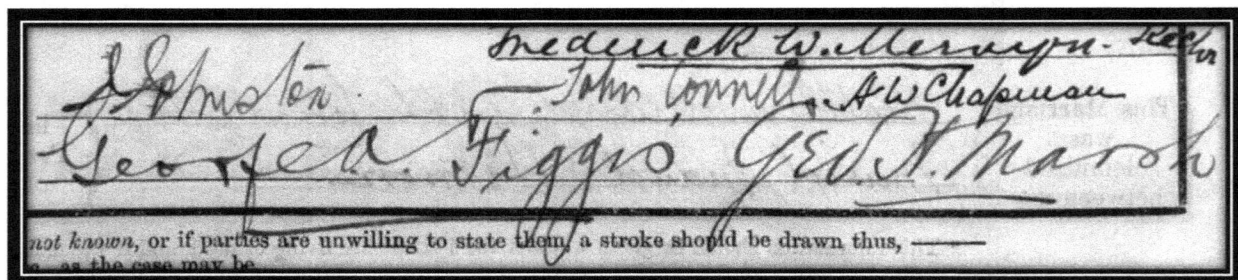

George Alexander Figgis (father):

Residence - 35 Lower Mount Pleasant Avenue - January 8, 1869

Occupation - Clerk in Bank of Ireland - January 8, 1869

- Gulielmo Figgis & Margaret Connor

  o Margaret Figgis – bapt. 27 Apr 1851 (Baptism, **Rathmines Parish (RC)**)

- John Figgis & Elizabeth Bradley – 27 Feb 1829 (Marriage, **St. Peter Parish**)

John Figgis (husband):

Residence - Camden Street, St. Peter's Parish - February 27, 1829

Elizabeth Bradley (wife):

Residence - Fitzwilliam Street - February 27, 1829

Figgis Surname Ireland: 1600s to 1900s

- John Samuel Figgis & Mary Figgis

    o John Albert Figgis – b. 9 Feb 1860, bapt. 1 Jul 1860 (Baptism, **St. Mary Parish**)

John Samuel Figgis (father):

> **Residence - 6 Dominick Street - July 1, 1860**

> **Occupation - Gentleman - July 1, 1860**

- Samuel Figgis & Elizabeth Hilchcoch – 19 Nov 1818 (Marriage, **St. Catherine Parish**)

Samuel Figgis (husband):

> **Residence - St. Michael's Parish - November 19, 1818**

Elizabeth Hilchcoch (wife):

> **Residence - St. Catherine Parish - November 19, 1818**

Wedding Witnesses:

John Davis & James Figgis

- Samuel Figgis & Mary Figgis

    o Thomas Frederick Figgis – b. 17 Apr 1869, bapt. 24 Jun 1869 (Baptism, **St. Peter Parish**)

Signature:

Samuel Figgis (father):

> **Residence - 94 Leinster Road - June 24, 1869**

> **Occupation - Merchant - June 24, 1869**

- Samuel Figgis & Unknown

  o John Samuel Figgis & Mary Dorothea Foster – 28 Oct 1847 (Marriage, **St. Peter Parish**)

Signatures:

John Samuel Figgis (son):

   Residence - Longford, Temple Michael Parish - October 28, 1847

   Occupation - Gentleman - October 28, 1847

Mary Dorothea Foster, daughter of Thomas Foster (daughter-in-law):

   Residence - Haddington Road, St. Peter Parish - October 28, 1847

Thomas Foster (father):

   Occupation - Gentleman

Samuel Figgis (father):

   Occupation - Glover

Wedding Witnesses:

William Foster & Alexander G. Figgis

Signatures:

Figgis Surname Ireland: 1600s to 1900s

o   Alexander Goudge Figgis, b. 1821, bur. 11 Nov 1854 (Burial, **St. Nicholas Without Parish**) & Jane
Cecilia Geary (1st Marriage) – 14 Nov 1851 (Marriage, **St. Peter Parish**)

Signatures:

Signatures (Marriage):

■ Elizabeth Adelaide Figgis – b. 10 Nov 1852, bapt. 29 Dec 1852 (Baptism, **St. Mary Parish**)

Alexander Goudge Figgis (son):

Residence - 55 Capel Street - November 14, 1851

December 29, 1852

Caroline Row - Before November 11, 1854

Occupation - Gentleman - November 14, 1851

Commercial Traveller - December 29, 1852

Age at Death - 33 years

Jane Cecilia Geary, daughter of William Geary (daughter-in-law):

Residence - 13 De Gray Terrace Haddington Road - November 14, 1851

Relationship Status at Marriage - minor

Hurst

William Geary (father):

Signature:

Occupation - Professor of Music

Samuel Figgis (father):

Occupation - Merchant

Wedding Witnesses:

William Geary & James Parker

Signatures:

- o Jane Cecilia Geary Figgis (2nd Marriage) & John Kirkland – 20 Feb 1860 (Marriage, **St. Peter Parish**)

Signatures:

Figgis Surname Ireland: 1600s to 1900s

Jane Cecilia Geary Figgis (daughter-in-law):

    Residence - 35 Harcourt Street - February 20, 1860

    Relationship Status at Marriage - widow

John Kirkland, son of William Kirkland (son-in-law):

    Residence - Rathgar - February 20, 1860

    Occupation - Bookkeeper - February 20, 1860

William Kirkland (father):

    Occupation - Merchant

William Geary (father):

    Occupation - Professor of Music

Wedding Witnesses:

Gustaves L. Geary & Frederick L. Morgan

Signatures:

- o Elizabeth Figgis & John Wallis – 23 Feb 1854 (Marriage, **St. Mary Parish**)

Signatures:

Elizabeth Figgis (daughter):

   Residence - 53 Capel Street - February 23, 1854

John Wallis, son of Thomas Wallis (son-in-law):

   Residence - Prospect Glasnevin - February 23, 1854

Thomas Wallis (father):

   Occupation - Builder

Samuel Figgis (father):

   Occupation - Glover

Wedding Witnesses:

Thomas Figgis

Signature:

- Thomas Figgis & Mary Anne Keene – 22 Apr 1819 (Marriage, **St. Peter Parish**)

Figgis Surname Ireland: 1600s to 1900s

- Thomas Gilbart Figgis & Unknown

Signature:

  - Jane Figgis & Edward Hill – 24 Apr 1845 (Marriage, **St. Peter Parish**)

Signatures:

Jane Figgis (daughter):

  Residence - 33 Richmond Street South - April 24, 1845

Edward Hill, son of Daniel Hill (son-in-law):

  Residence - Richmond Street - April 24, 1845

  Occupation - Independent Clergyman - April 24, 1845

Daniel Hill (father):

  Occupation - Gentleman

Thomas Figgis (father):

  Occupation - Merchant

Wedding Witnesses:

Thomas G. Figgis & John T. Purcell

Signatures:

- o Samuel Figgis & Mary Anne Cuttle – 6 Sep 1860 (Marriage, **St. Peter Parish**)

Signatures:

- Elizabeth Mary Figgis – b. 24 Aug 1862, bapt. 11 Jan 1863 (Baptism, **St. Peter Parish**)

- Catherine Eva Figgis – b. 16 Aug 1867, bapt. 28 Nov 1867 (Baptism, **St. Peter Parish**)

- William Fernsley (F e r n s l e y) Figgis – b. 11 Jan 1874, bapt. 6 Feb 1874 (Baptism, **Harold's Cross Parish**)

- Edward Allen Keane Figgis – b. 9 Feb 1876, bapt. 7 Apr 1876 (Baptism, **Harold's Cross Parish**)

- Helen Margaret Figgis – b. 4 Jun 1880, bapt. 25 Jun 1880 (Baptism, **Harold's Cross Parish**)

Figgis Surname Ireland: 1600s to 1900s

Samuel Figgis (son):

    Residence - 55 Richmond Street South - September 6, 1860

        Garville Avenue - January 11, 1863

        Brighton Avenue, Rathgar - November 28, 1867

    No 77 Leinster Road, Rathmines - February 6, 1874

        April 7, 1876

        June 25, 1880

    Occupation - Publisher - September 6, 1860

        Clerk - January 11, 1863

        November 28, 1867

        Bookseller & Publisher - February 6, 1874

        April 7, 1876

        June 25, 1880

Mary Anne Cuttle, daughter of Thomas Henry Cuttle (daughter-in-law):

    Residence - Mill Mount, Mullingar - September 6, 1860

Thomas Henry Cuttle (father):

Signature:

    Occupation - Agent

Thomas Figgis (father):

    Occupation - Merchant

Wedding Witnesses:

T. H. Cuttle & Thomas Gilbart Figgis

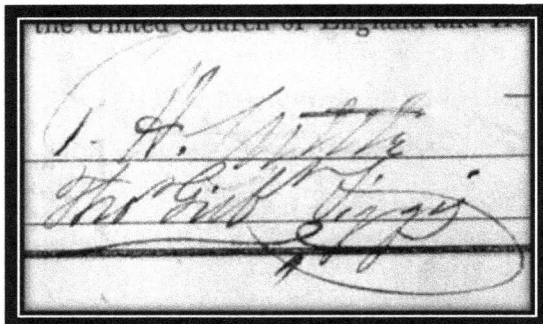

Signatures:

- o   Thomas Gilbart Figgis & Unknown

Signature:

- ▪ Margaret Hope Figgis & Duncan Frederick Basden – 23 Apr 1885 (Marriage, **Rathmines Parish**)

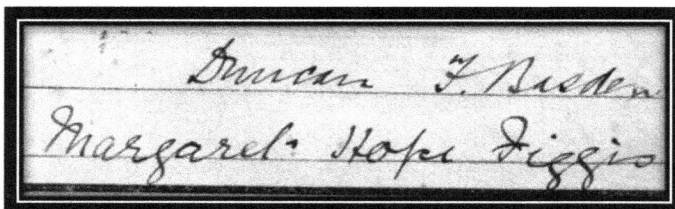

Signatures:

Margaret Hope Figgis (daughter):

   Residence - 40 Grosvenor Square - April 23, 1885

Duncan Frederick Basden, son of Edward Weeks Spencer Basden (son-in-law):

   Residence - Nottigham - April 23, 1885

   Occupation - Accountant - April 23, 1885

Edward Weeks Spencer Basden (father):

    Occupation - Esquire

Thomas Gilbart Figgis (father):

    Occupation - Merchant

Wedding Witnesses:

Isabel Francis Figgis & Alfred James Basden

Signatures:

- Arthur Wellesley Lenox Figgis & Adeline Wilson Hewitt – 23 Jun 1885 (Marriage, **Rathmines Parish**)

Signatures:

Arthur Wellsley Lenox Figgis (son):

    Residence - 40 Grosvenor Square - June 25, 1885

    Occupation - Corn Broker - June 23, 1885

Adeline Wilson Hewitt, daughter of Gustavus Wilson (daughter-in-law):

    Residence - 164 Rathgar Road - June 23, 1885

    Relationship Status at Marriage - widow

Gustavus Wilson (father):

    Occupation - Merchant

Thomas Gilbart Figgis (father):

    Occupation - Merchant

Wedding Witnesses:

Mary Wilson & Charles Figgis

Signatures:

- Isabel Frances Figgis & Harold Stevens Basden – 20 Dec 1892 (Marriage, **Rathmines Parish**)

Signature:

Signatures (Marriage):

Isabel Frances Figgis (daughter):

    Residence - 40 Grosvenor Square, Rathmines - December 20, 1892

    Occupation - Gentlewoman - December 20, 1892

Harold Stevens Basden, son of Edward Weeks Spencer Basden (son-in-law):

    Residence - 4 Cannon Place, Hampstead, Heath, London - December 20, 1892

    Occupation - Medical Student - December 20. 1892

He is the brother to Duncan Frederick Basden.

Figgis Surname Ireland: 1600s to 1900s

Edward Weeks Spencer Basden (father):

    Residence - H. M. Civil Service

Thomas Gilbart Figgis (father):

    Occupation - Merchant

Wedding Witnesses:

Ethel Figgis & Frank F. Figgis

Signatures:

- Lucy Ethel Figgis & John Leslie Collins – 26 Jun 1895 (Marriage, **Rathmines Parish**)

Signatures:

Lucy Ethel Figgis (daughter):

    Residence - 40 Grosvenor Square, Rathmines - June 26, 1895

John Leslie Collins, son of Joseph Collins (son-in-law):

    Residence - 26 Grosvenor Square - June 26, 1895

    Occupation - Civil Service - June 26, 1895

Joseph Collins (father):

    Occupation - Bankruptcy Court

Thomas Gilbart Figgis (father):

    Occupation - Esquire

Wedding Witnesses:

Theodore G. Figgis & Mary C. Figgis

Signatures:

Thomas Gilbart Figgis (father):

>   **Residence - 40 Grosvenor Square, Rathmines**

>   **Occupation - Merchant**

>   **Esquire**

- William Figgis & Margaret Connor

  o   Margaret Figgis – bapt. 27 Apr 1851 (Baptism, **Rathmines Parish (RC)**)

- William Figgis & Mary Unknown

  o   Louisa Figgis – b. 10 Jan 1836, bapt. 24 Jan 1836 (Baptism, **St. Peter Parish**)

William Figgis (father):

>   **Residence - No 5 Long Lane - January 24, 1836**

- William Figgis & Unknown

  o   Edmund Johnstone Figgis & Frances Anne Nicks – 21 Oct 1847 (Marriage, **St. Mary Parish**)

Signature:

Figgis Surname Ireland: 1600s to 1900s

Signatures (Marriage):

- Edmund Johnston Figgis – b. 24 May 1849, bapt. 3 Jul 1849 (Baptism, **St. Peter Parish**)

- Henry Wingfield Figgis, b. 11 May 1848, bapt. 19 Jul 1848 (Baptism, **St. Peter Parish**) & Emily
  Harris – 4 Apr 1871 (Marriage, **St. Peter Parish**)

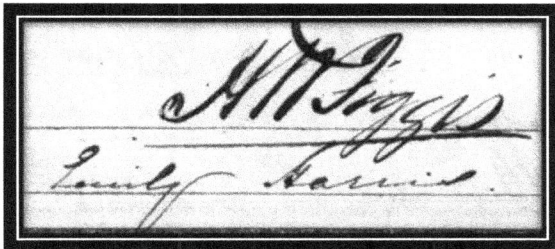

Signatures:

Henry Wingfield Figgis (son of Edmund Johnston Figgis & Frances Anne Nicks):

　　Residence - 2 Palmerston Park - April 4, 1871

　　Occupation - Merchant - April 4, 1871

Emily Harris, daughter of Robert Russell Harris (daughter-in-law):

　　Residence - 28 Livester Road - April 4, 1871

Robert Russell Harris (father):

　　Occupation - Colonel in the Army

Edmund Johnstone Figgis (father):

　　Occupation - Merchant

Wedding Witnesses:

Edmund Johnstone Figgis & R. R. Harris

Signatures:

- Arthur William Figgis – b. 15 Jun 1850, bapt. 17 Jul 1850 (Baptism, **St. Peter Parish**)

- Frances Anne Figgis – b. 24 Apr 1852, bapt. 11 May 1852 (Baptism, **St. Peter Parish**)

- Robert Edward Figgis – b. 30 May 1853, bapt. 7 Jul 1853 (Baptism, **St. Peter Parish**)

- Florence Figgis – b. 22 Jan 1863, bapt. 30 Jan 1863 (Baptism, **St. Peter Parish**)

Edmund Johnstone Figgis (son):

Residence - 13 Essex Street - October 21, 1847

30 Harold's Cross - July 19, 1848

July 3, 1849

42 Harold's Cross - July 17, 1850

No 1 Leinster Road, Rathmines - May 11, 1852

July 17, 1853

Growen Square, Leinster Road - January 30, 1863

Occupation - Gentleman - October 21, 1847

Merchant - July 19, 1848

July 3, 1849

July 17, 1850

Stationer - May 11, 1852

July 17, 1853

Commercial Traveller - January 30, 1863

Figgis Surname Ireland: 1600s to 1900s

Frances Anne Nicks, daughter of Richard Wingfield Nicks (daughter-in-law):

Residence - 9 Bachelor's Walk - October 21, 1847

Richard Wingfield Nicks (father):

Occupation - Gentleman

William Figgis (father):

Occupation - Gentleman

- William Henry Figgis & Mary Figgis

  o Mary Figgis – b. 31 Mar 1856, bapt. 23 Jun 1858 (Baptism, **St. Peter Parish**)

  o Anne Jane Figgis – b. 11 Mar 1858, bapt. 23 Jun 1858 (Baptism, **St. Peter Parish**)

  o Thomas Figgis – b. 29 Jul 1859, bapt. 29 Jan 1860 (Baptism, **St. Peter Parish**)

William Henry Figgis (father):

Residence - 7 Mount Pleasant Avenue - June 23, 1858

    5 Wharton Terrace - January 29, 1860

Occupation - Bookkeeper - June 23, 1858

    January 29, 1860

Individual Births/Baptisms

None were listed

Individual Burials

- Elizabeth Figgis – b. Oct 1823, bur. 7 Mar 1825 (Burial, **St. Nicholas Without Parish**)

Elizabeth Figgis (deceased):

>   Residence - Rathmines - Before March 7, 1825

>   Age at Death - 18 months

- Mary Figgis – bur. 7 Aug 1809 (Burial, **St. Nicholas Without Parish**)

Mary Figgis (deceased):

>   Residence - Charlemont Street - Before August 7, 1809

- Samuel Figgis – b. 1752, bur. 18 Apr 1825 (Burial, **St. Nicholas Without Parish**)

Samuel Figgis (deceased):

>   Residence - Charlemont Street - Before April 18, 1825

>   Age at Death - 73 years

- Samuel Figgis – b. Jul 1825, bur. 6 Sep 1826 (Burial, **St. Nicholas Without Parish**)

Samuel Figgis (deceased):

>   Residence - Charlemont Street - Before September 6, 1826

>   Age at Death - 10 months

Individual Marriages

- Elizabeth Figgis & John Nathaniel St. Georges – 30 Jul 1841 (Marriage, **St. Peter Parish**)

  o John St. Georges & Elizabeth Margaret Purcell – 10 Oct 1872 (Marriage, **St. Peter Parish**)

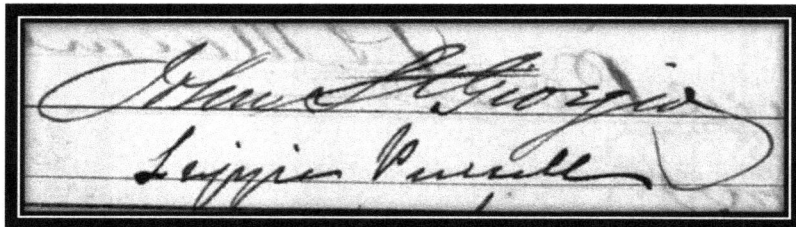

Signatures:

John St. Georges (son):

   Residence - 8 Adelaide Road - October 10, 1872

   Occupation - Book Seller - October 10, 1872

Elizabeth Margaret Purcell, daughter of John Theobald Purcell and Sarah Figgis (daughter-in-law):

   Residence - Ontario Terrace - October 10, 1872

John Theobald Purcell (father):

   Occupation - Solicitor

John Nathaniel St. Georges (father):

   Occupation - Esquire

Figgis Surname Ireland: 1600s to 1900s

Wedding Witnesses:

Edward Figgis & Mary A. Purcell

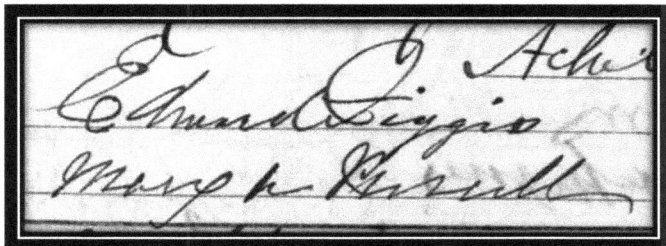

Signatures:

Elizabeth Figgis (mother):

> Residence - Richmond Hill - July 30, 1841

John Nathaniel St. Georges (father):

> Residence - Ranelagh - July 30, 1841

Wedding Witnesses:

John Purcell & Sarah Figgis

- Jane Esther Figgis & James Gibbon Wilson – 25 Nov 1828 (Marriage, **St. Peter Parish**)

Jane Esther Figgis (wife):

> Residence - Charlemont Mall - November 25, 1828

James Gibbon Wilson, son of Gibbon Wilson (son-in-law):

> Residence - Jervis Street, St. Mary's Parish - November 25, 1828

Wedding Witnesses:

William Figgis & Richard Wilson

- Mary Figgis & Richard John Hick – 16 May 1835 (Marriage, **St. Mary Parish**)

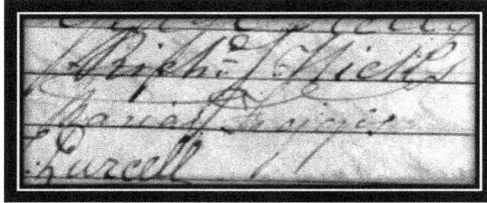

Signatures:

Mary Figgis (wife):

Residence - St. Mary Parish - May 16, 1835

Richard John Hick (husband):

Residence - St. Peter Parish, Dublin - Mary 16, 1835

Wedding Witnesses:

John T. Purcell & Mary Hicks

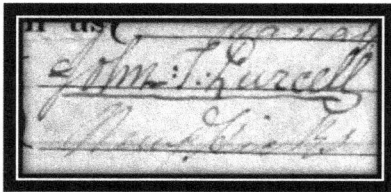

Signatures:

- Mary Figgis & Thomas Gilbart – 11 Aug 1821 (Marriage, **St. Peter Parish**)

Mary Figgis (wife):

Residence - St. Peter Parish - August 11, 1821

Thomas Gilbart (husband):

Residence - City of London - August 11, 1821

Wedding Witnesses:

Samuel Figgis & Thomas Figgis

Figgis Surname Ireland: 1600s to 1900s

- Mary Figgis & William Goodshaw – 27 Dec 1823 (Marriage, **St. Peter Parish**)

Mary Figgis (wife):

   Residence - St. Peter Parish - December 27, 1823

William Goodshaw (husband):

   Residence - Leixlip Parish, Co. Kildare - December 27, 1823

- Sarah Figgis & John Sargeant

   o Isabel Sargeant – bapt. 15 Nov 1833 (Baptism, **St. Catherine Parish** (RC))

   o Julia Sargeant – bapt. 27 Jan 1836 (Baptism, **St. Catherine Parish** (RC))

- Sarah Figgis & John Theobald Purcell – 30 Apr 1831 (Marriage, **St. Peter Parish**)

   o Elizabeth Margaret Purcell & John St. Georges – 10 Oct 1872 (Marriage, **St. Peter Parish**)

Sarah Figgis (mother):

   Residence - Peter Place - April 30, 1831

   Occupation - Spinster - April 30, 1831

John Theobald Purcell (father):

   Residence - Windy Arbour, Taney Parish - April 30, 1831

   Occupation - Esquire - April 30, 1831

Wedding Witnesses:

William Figgis & William Purcell

Name Variations

Includes Latin and Abbreviated forms of names found in the original documents.

Abigail = Abigale, Abigall

Anne = Ann, Anna, Annae

Bartholomew = Barth, Bartholmeus, Bartholomeo

Benjamin = Benj

Bridget = Birgis, Brigid, Brigida, Bridgit

Catherine = Catharine, Catharina, Catharinae, Catherina, Cath, Catha, Cathae, Cathe, Cathn, Kate

Charles = Carolus, Charls, Chas

Christopher = Christoph

Daniel = Danielem, Danielis

Edmund = Edmond

Edward = Ed, Edwd

Eleanor = Eleo, Eleonora, Elinor, Ellenor

Elizabeth = Betty, Elisa, Elisabeth, Eliz, Eliza, Elizab, Elizh, Elizth

Ellen = Elena, Ellena

Emily= Emilia

Esther = Essie, Ester

Francis = Fransicum

George = Geo, Georg, Georgius

Grace = Gratiae

Gulielmo = Guil, Guillelmi, Gulielmum, Guillelmus, Gulmi

Figgis Surname Ireland: 1600s to 1900s

Harold = Harry

Helen = Helena

Honor = Hanora, Honora

Hugh = Hew

James = Jacobi, Jacobus, Jas

Jane = Joanna

Jeanne = Jeannae, Joannae

Joan = Johanna, Joney

John = Jno, Joannem, Joannes, Johannis

Joseph = Jos

Leticia = Letitia, Lettice, Letticia

Margaret = Margarita, Margaritae, Margeret, Marget, Margt

Martha = Marthae

Mary = Maria, My

Mary Anne = Marianna, Marianne, Maryanne

Michael = Michaelis, Michl

Patrick = Pat, Patt, Patk, Patricii, Patricius

Richard = Ricardi, Ricardus, Rich, Richd

Thomas = Thom, Thomae, Thoms, Thos, Ths

Timothy = Timotheus, Timy

Valentine = Val, Valentinae, Valentinus

William = Wil, Will, Willm, Wm

Notes

Notes

Notes

Notes

Notes

Notes

Index

Figgis Surname Ireland: 1600s to 1900s

About The Author

Donovan Hurst graduated from San Diego State University with a Bachelor of Arts in the major field of studies of History and a minor in the field of studies of Anthropology. He is a current member of The General Society of Mayflower Descendants and has been conducting genealogical research for over 10 years tracing back his ancestors to their ancestral homelands in Denmark, England, France, Germany, Ireland, Norway, and Scotland.

www.ingramcontent.com/pod-product-compliance
Lightning Source LLC
Chambersburg PA
CBHW081204270326
41930CB00014B/3296